EASY PIANO

Disney
Olaf's FROZEN ADVENTURE

SONGS FROM THE ORIGINAL SOUNDTRACK

ISBN 978-1-5400-1381-1

Wonderland Music Company, Inc.

DISTRIBUTED BY

HAL•LEONARD®

7777 W. BLUEMOUND RD. P.O. BOX 13819 MILWAUKEE, WI 53213

In Australia Contact:
Hal Leonard Australia Pty. Ltd.
4 Lentara Court
Cheltenham, Victoria, 3192 Australia
Email: ausadmin@halleonard.com.au

Visit Hal Leonard Online at
www.halleonard.com

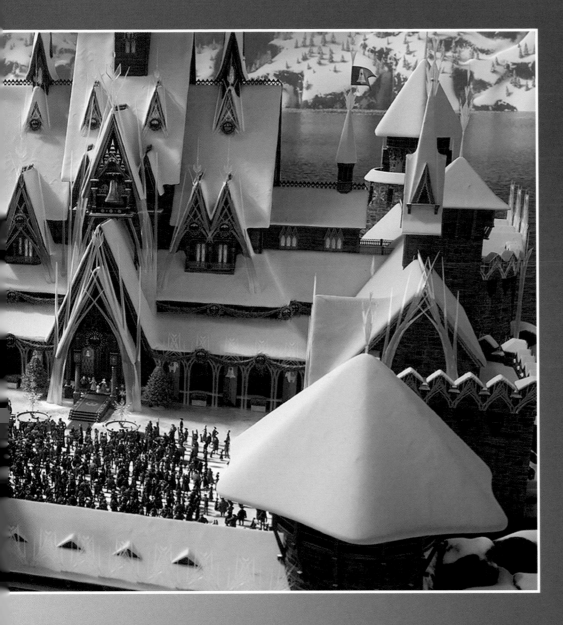

RING IN THE SEASON

Music and Lyrics by ELYSSA SAMSEL
and KATE ANDERSON

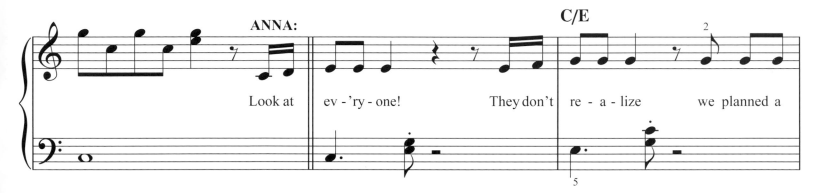

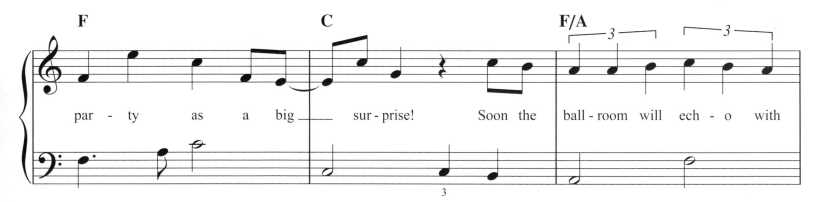

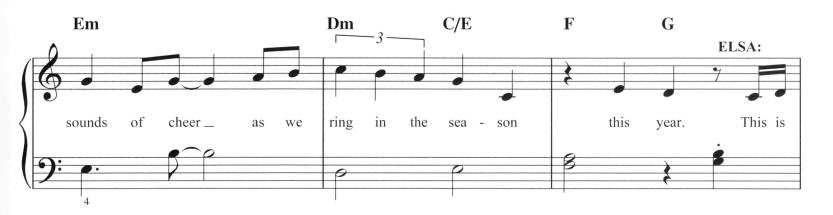

o - ver - due!   Got-ta   look   our   best!   I've   nev - er   been   so   nice-

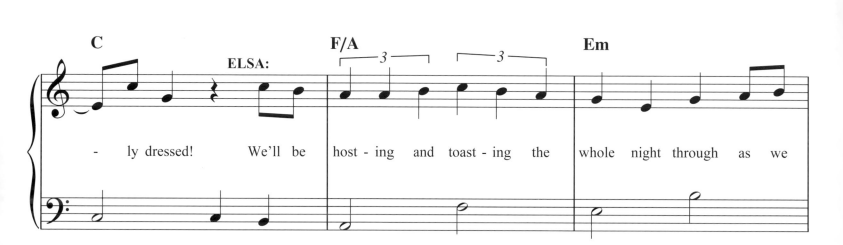

- ly   dressed!   We'll   be   host - ing   and   toast - ing   the   whole   night   through   as   we

ring   in   the   sea - son   with   you.   It's   the   first   Christ-mas   in   for-

ev - er   since   we   o - pened   up ___ the   gate. ___   And   it's   the

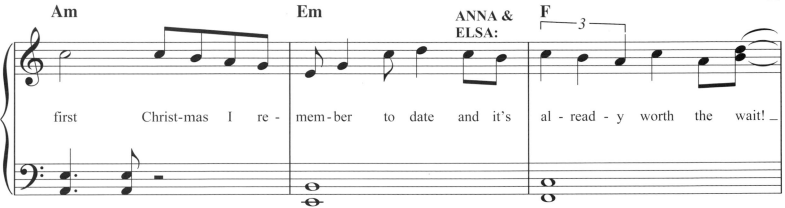

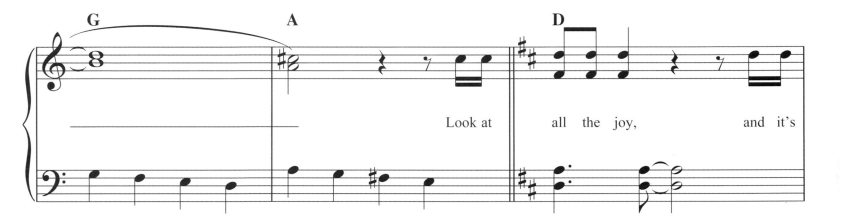

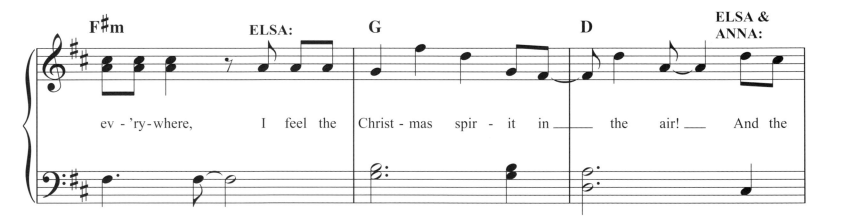

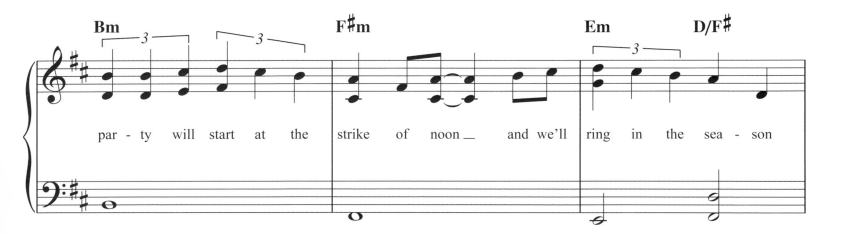

12

so soon.

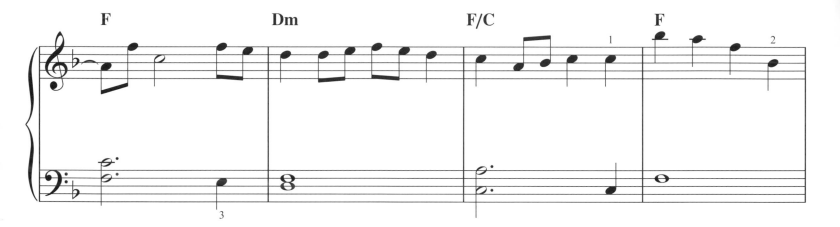

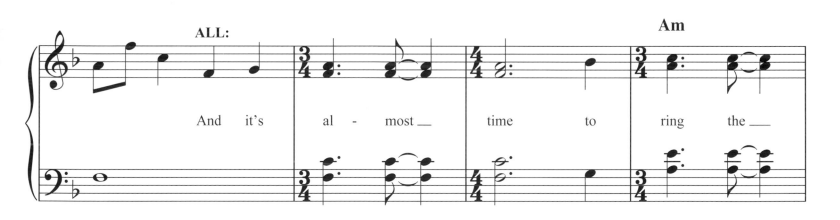

And it's al - most __ time to ring the __

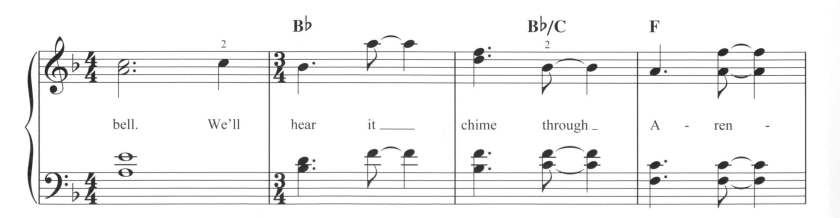

bell. We'll hear it ____ chime through _ A - ren -

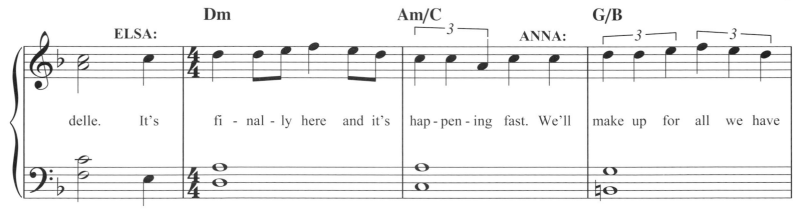

ELSA: delle. It's fi - nal - ly here and it's hap - pen - ing fast. We'll make up for all we have

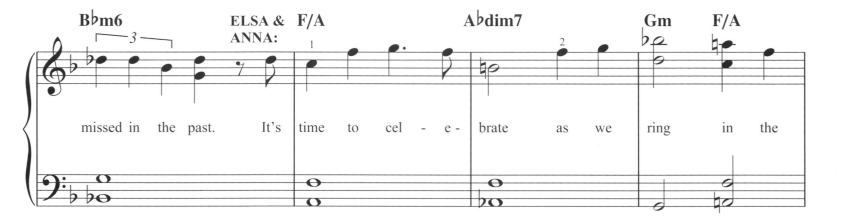

missed in the past. It's time to cel - e - brate as we ring in the

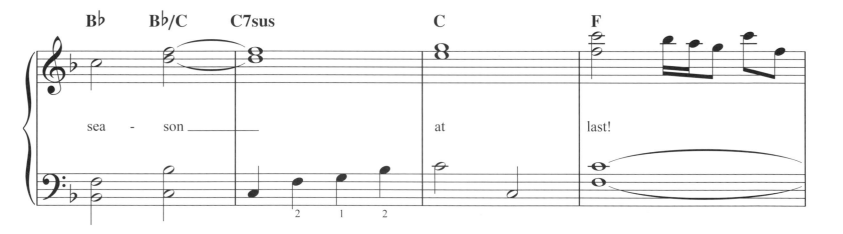

sea - son _____ at last!

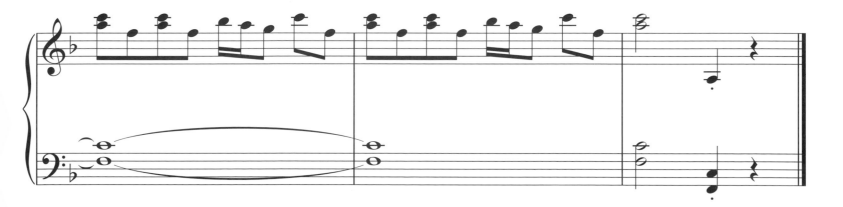

THE BALLAD OF FLEMMINGRAD

Music and Lyrics by ELYSSA SAMSEL
and KATE ANDERSON

Moderately fast

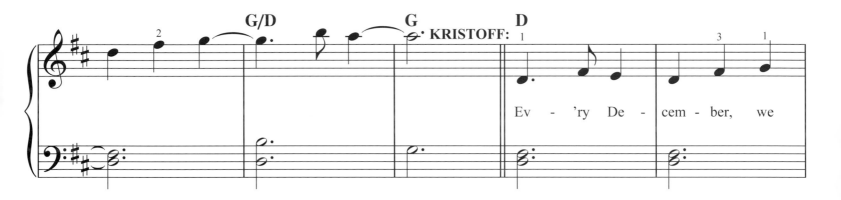

KRISTOFF: Ev - ’ry De - cem - ber, we

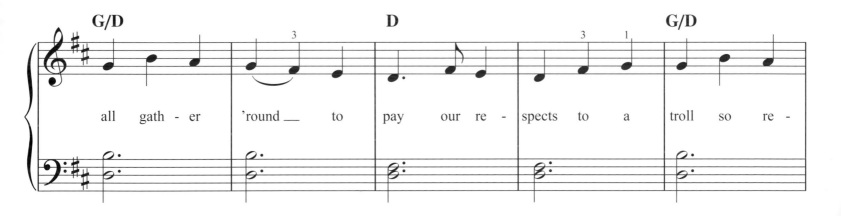

all gath - er ’round ___ to pay our re - spects to a troll so re -

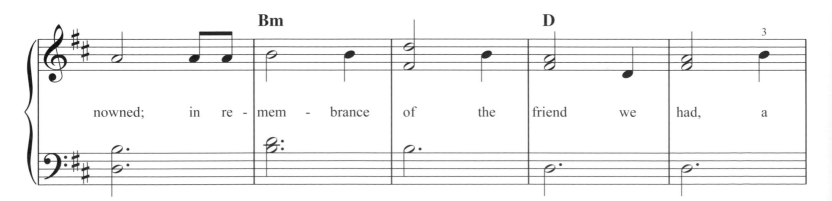

nowned; in re - mem - brance of the friend we had, a

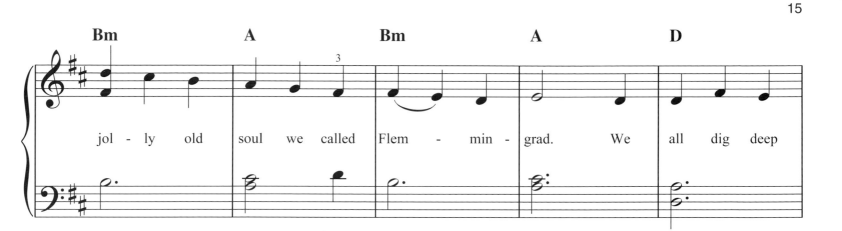

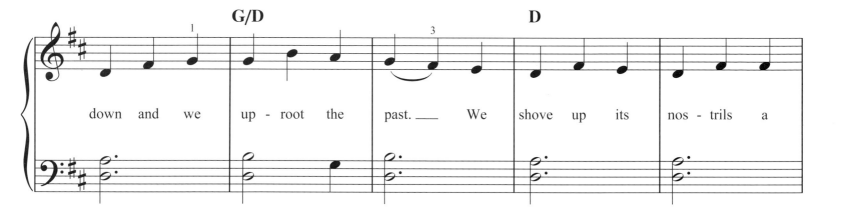

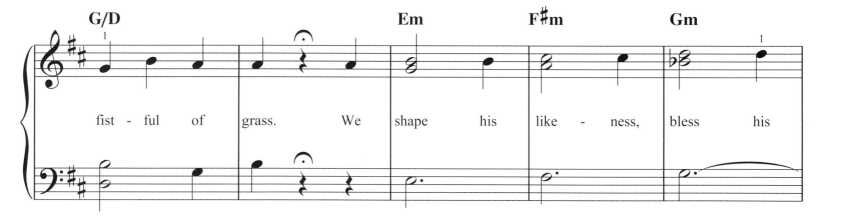

THAT TIME OF YEAR

Music and Lyrics by ELYSSA SAMSEL
and KATE ANDERSON

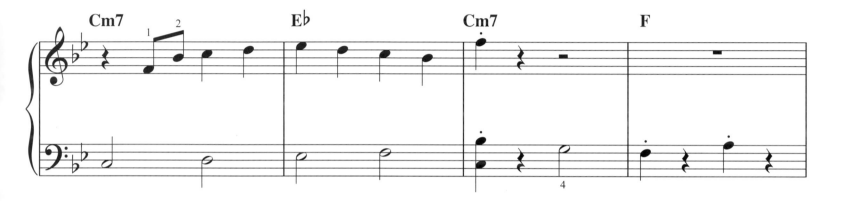

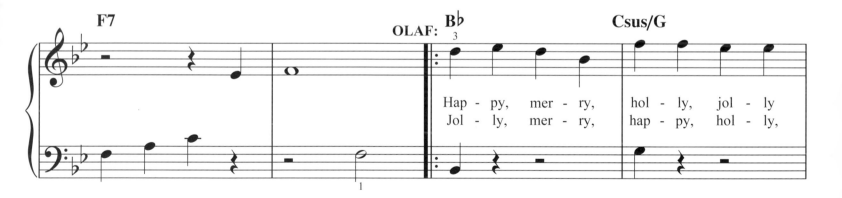

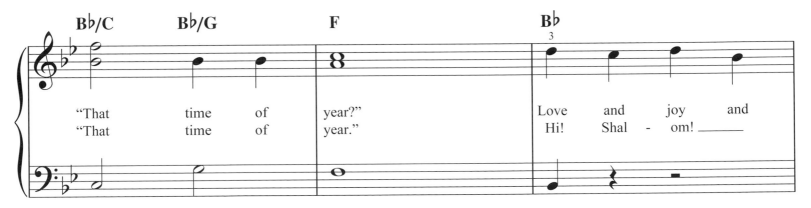

"That time of year?"
"That time of year."
Love and joy and
Hi! Shal - om! _____

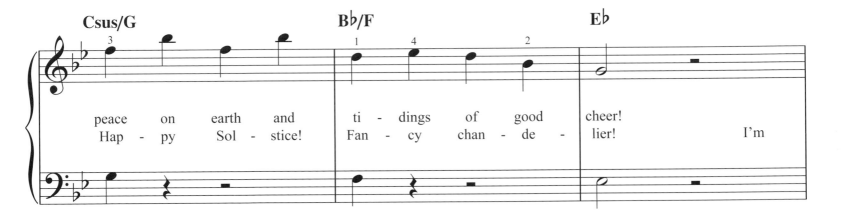

peace on earth and
Hap - py Sol - stice!
ti - dings of good
Fan - cy chan - de -
cheer!
lier! I'm

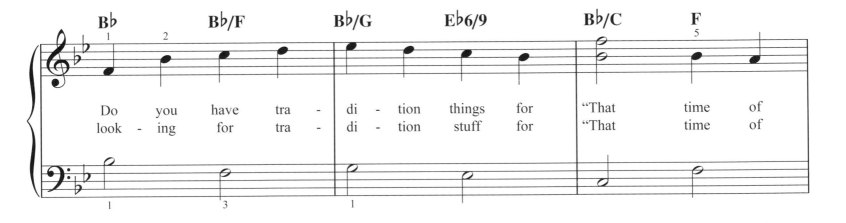

Do you have tra - di - tion things for
look - ing have for tra - di - tion stuff for
"That time of
"That time of

year?" **OLGA:** Well, we
year." **MR. ASELSON:** Well, we
hang up boughs of
make our dec - o - ra - tions out of
ev - er - green on

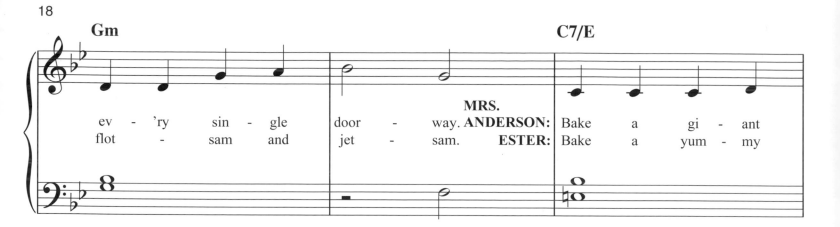

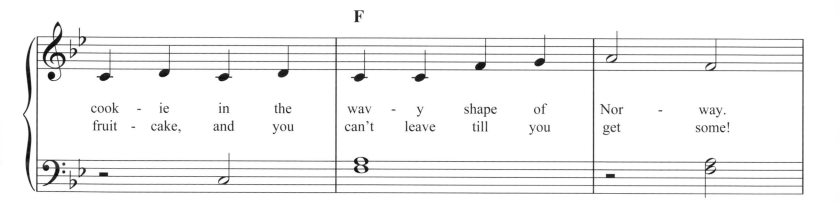

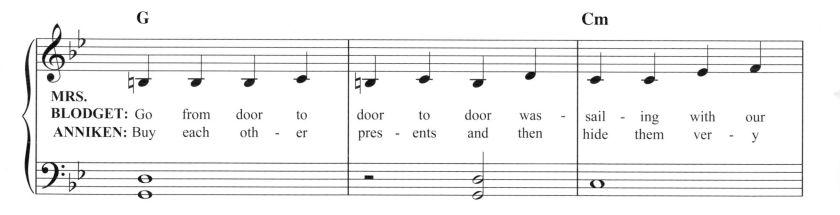

N.C.

bove an o - pen fi - re.
shim - my down your chim - ney.

A+

Spoken: That sounds safe!
Spoken: Breaking and entering okay on Christmas!

So,
Oh,

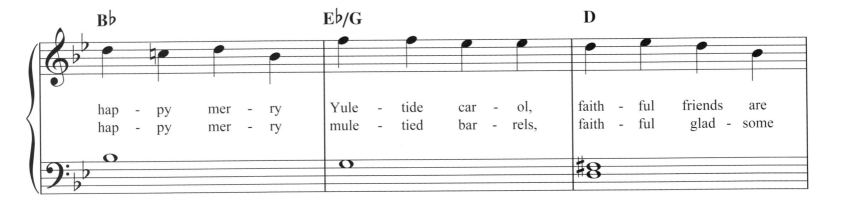

B♭   E♭/G   D

hap - py mer - ry Yule - tide car - ol, faith - ful friends are
hap - py mer - ry mule - tied bar - rels, faith - ful glad - some

Gm   C/E   Cm

dear.   Thanks for shar - ing what you do at "That
cheer.   Thanks for shar - ing what you do at "That

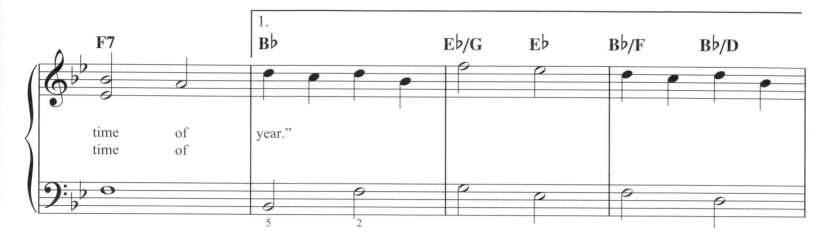

C7/E

INGRID:

mit - tens. Don't for - get the jam - mies that I

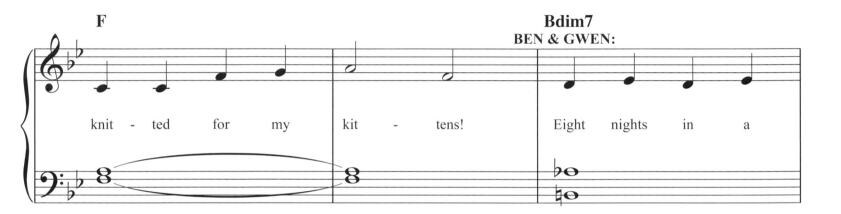

F

Bdim7

BEN & GWEN:

knit - ted for my kit - tens! Eight nights in a

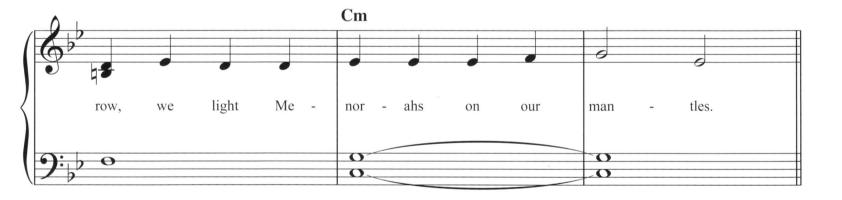

Cm

row, we light Me - nor - ahs on our man - tles.

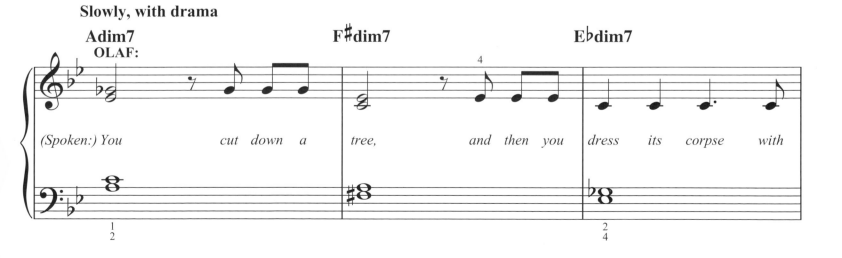

Slowly, with drama

Adim7

F#dim7

Ebdim7

OLAF:

(Spoken:) You cut down a tree, and then you dress its corpse with

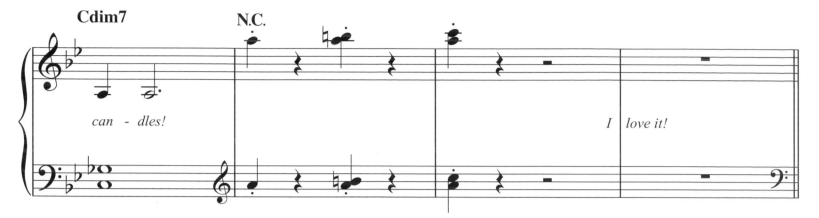

Cdim7   N.C.

can - dles!   *I love it!*

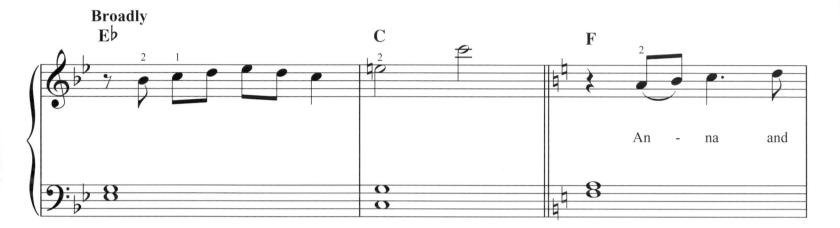

Broadly

Eb   C   F

An - na and

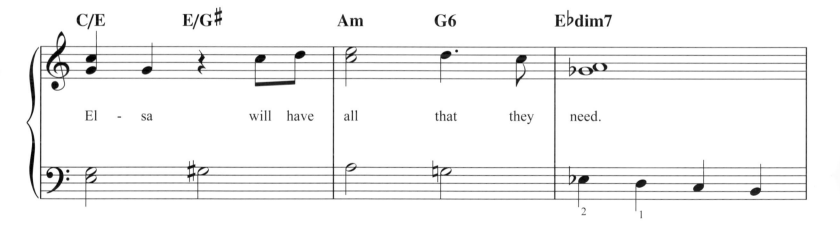

C/E   E/G#   Am   G6   Ebdim7

El - sa   will have   all   that   they   need.

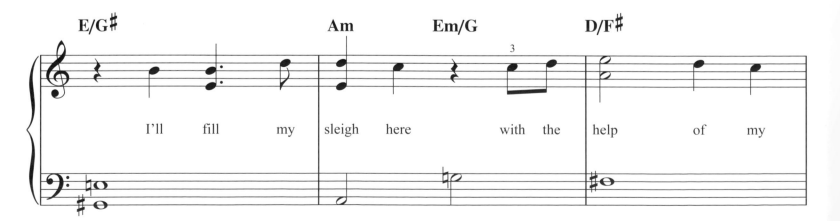

E/G#   Am   Em/G   D/F#

I'll   fill   my   sleigh here   with the   help   of   my

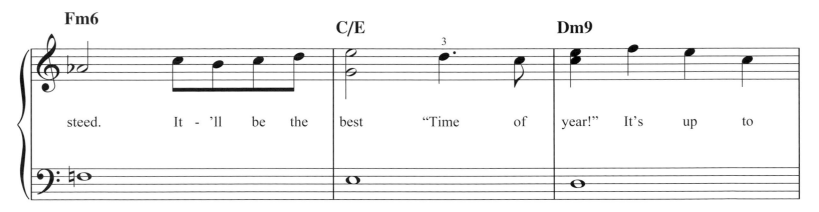

steed.   It - 'll   be   the   best   "Time   of   year!"   It's   up   to

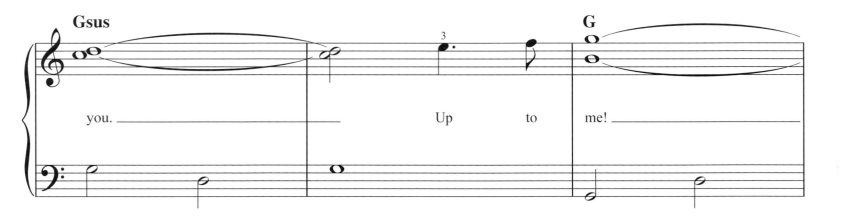

you. _____   Up   to   me! _____

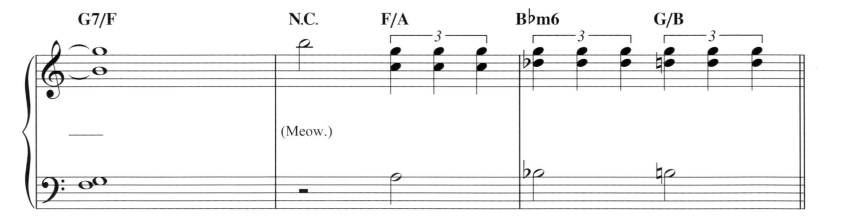

(Meow.)

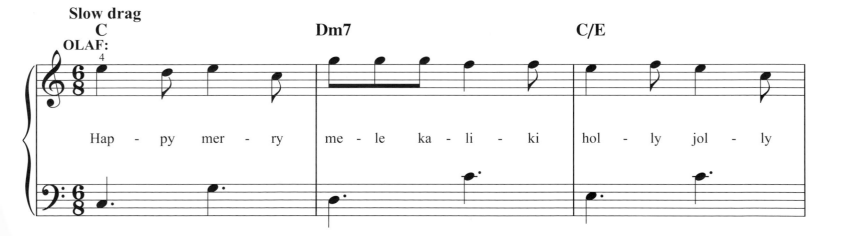

Hap - py   mer - ry   me - le - ka - li - ki   hol - ly   jol - ly

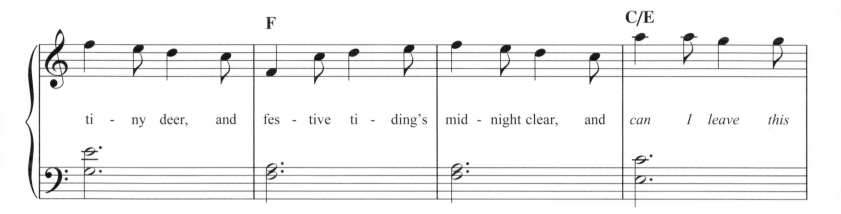

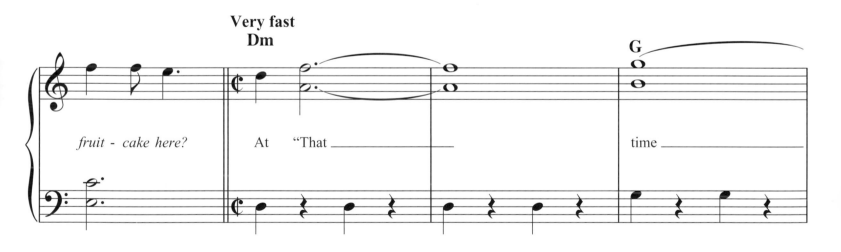

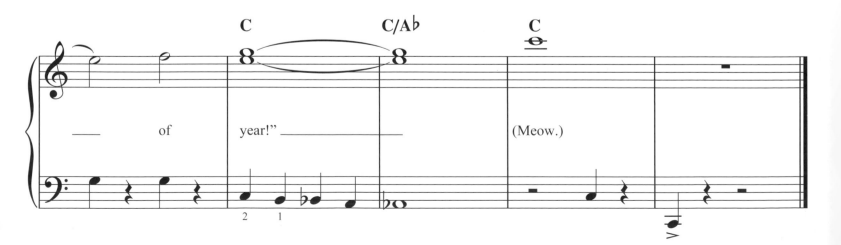

WHEN WE'RE TOGETHER

Music and Lyrics by ELYSSA SAMSEL
and KATE ANDERSON

Moderately, with a lilt

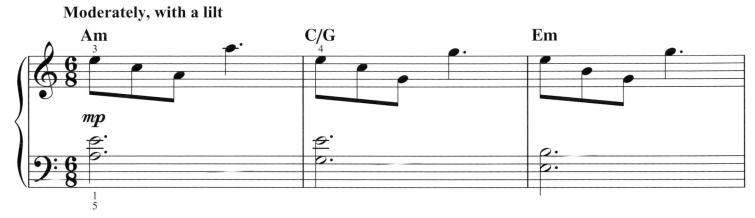

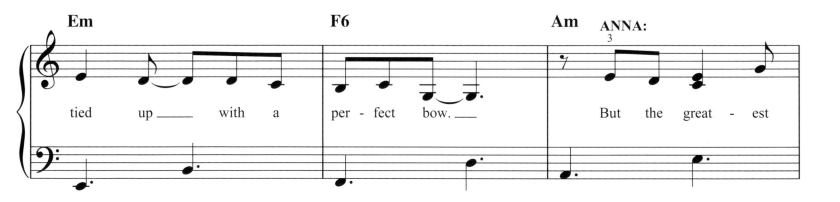

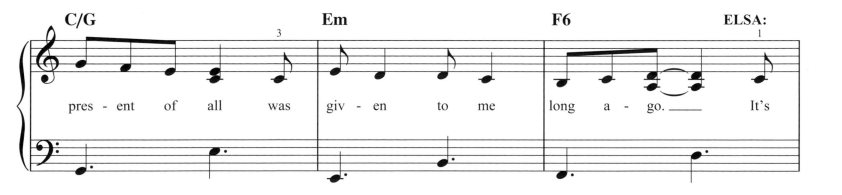

Am / **G6** / **F**

some - thing I would nev - er trade, it's the fam - ily that we've

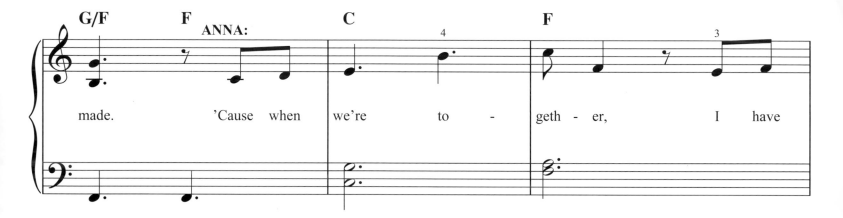

G/F / **F** ANNA: / **C** / **F**

made. 'Cause when we're to - geth - er, I have

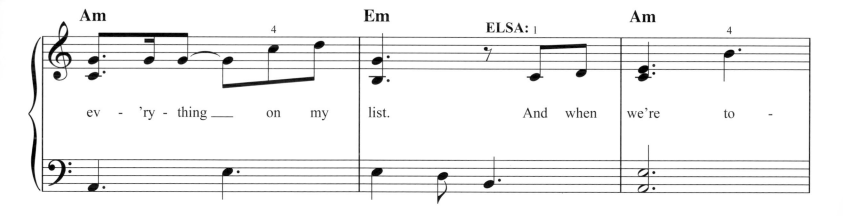

Am / **Em** / ELSA: / **Am**

ev - 'ry - thing___ on my list. And when we're to -

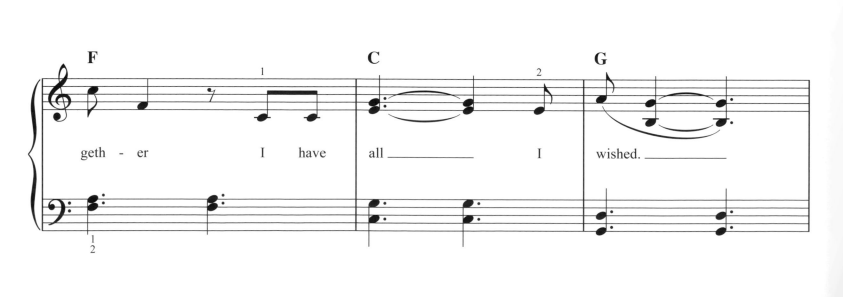

F / **C** / **G**

geth - er I have all _____ I wished. _____

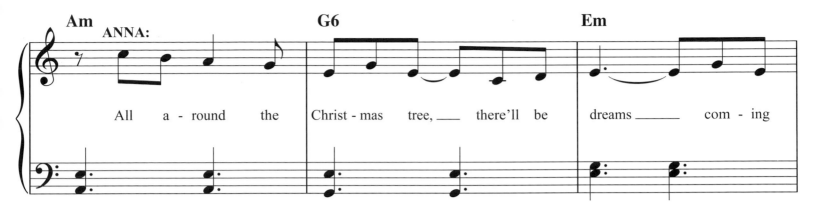

All a - round the Christ - mas tree, ___ there'll be dreams ___ com - ing

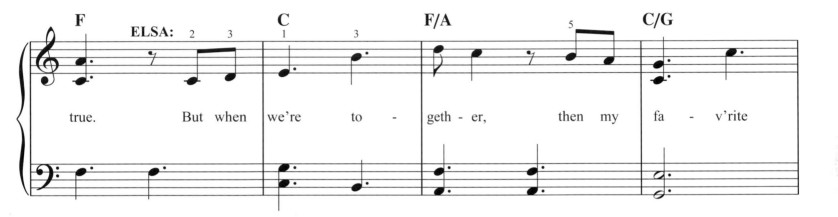

true. But when we're to - geth - er, then my fa - v'rite

gift is you. ___

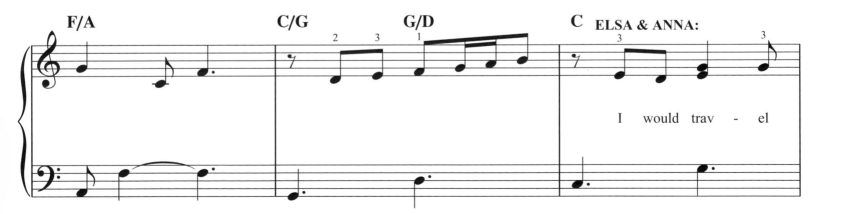

I would trav - el

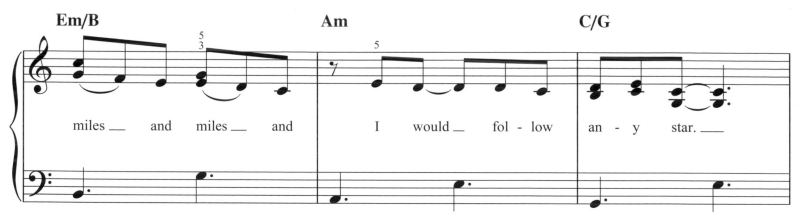

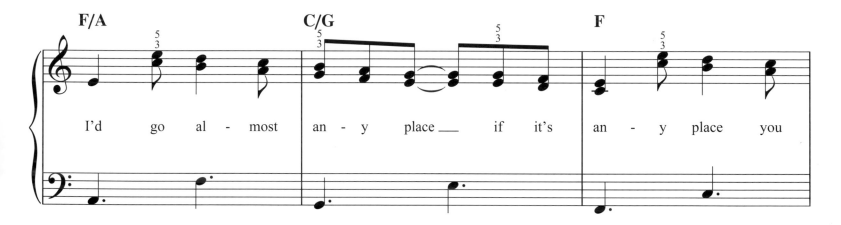

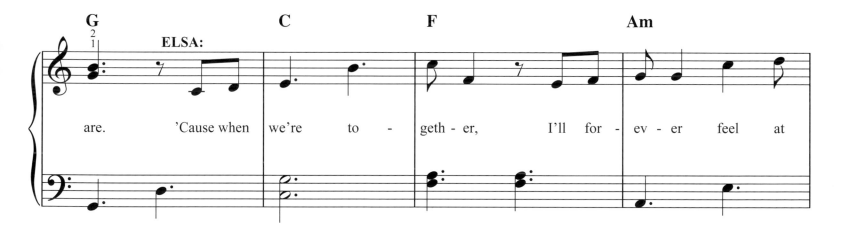

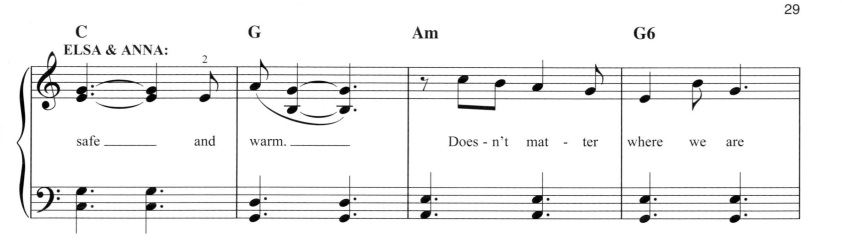

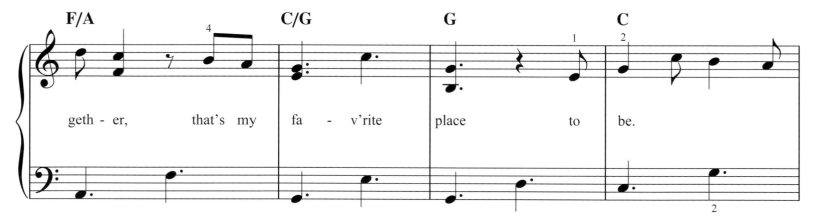

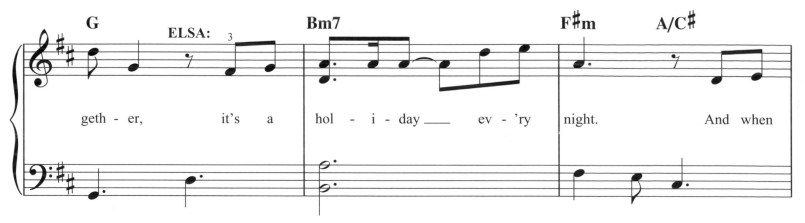

G   ELSA: Bm7   F#m   A/C#

geth - er,   it's   a   hol - i - day ____ ev - 'ry   night.   And when

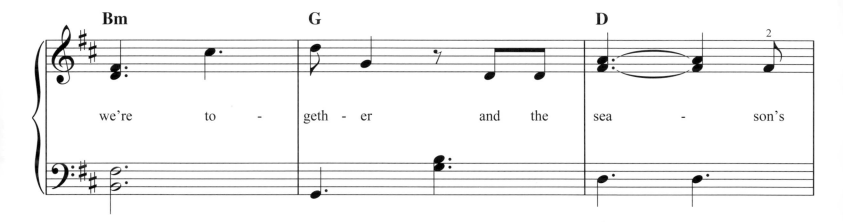

Bm   G   D

we're   to -   geth - er   and   the   sea -   son's

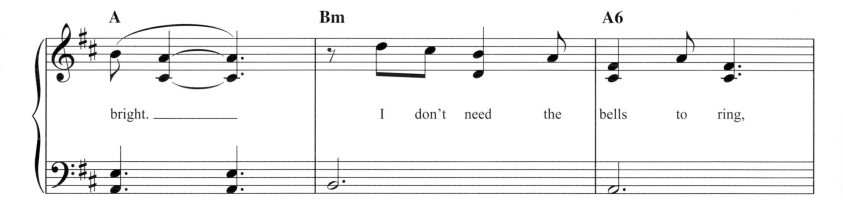

A   Bm   A6

bright. _____   I   don't   need   the   bells   to   ring,

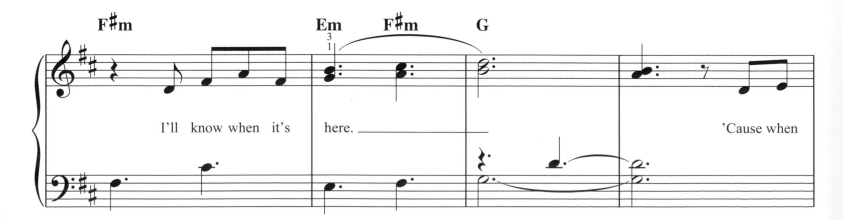

F#m   Em   F#m   G

I'll   know   when   it's   here. _____   'Cause when

we're to - geth - er, I could stay for - ev - er. And when

we're to - geth - er it's my fa - v'rite

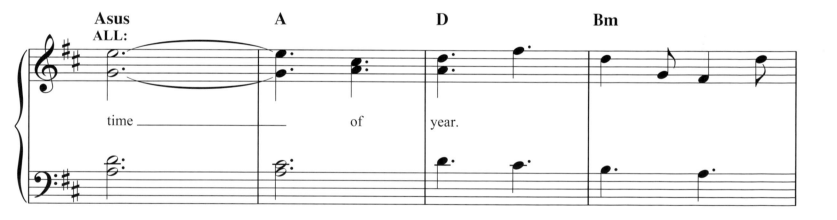

time _____ of year.

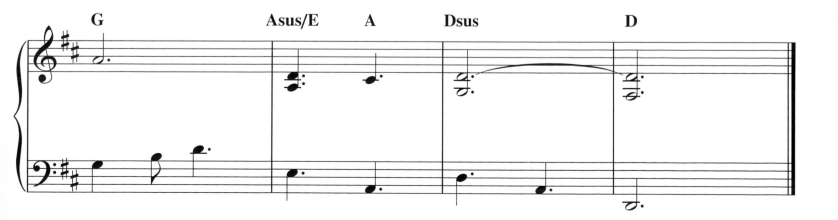